HOW BOOKS CAN SAVE DEMOCRACY

MICHAEL FISCHER

TRINITY UNIVERSITY PRESS
SAN ANTONIO, TEXAS

Trinity University Press
San Antonio, Texas 78212

Copyright © 2025 by Michael Fischer

All rights reserved. No part of this book may be reproduced in any form or by any electronic or mechanical means, including information storage and retrieval systems, without permission in writing from the publisher.

Book design by Anne Richmond Boston
Author photo by Jeri Krentz

ISBN 978-1-59534-321-5 paper
ISBN 978-1-59534-322-2 ebook

Trinity University Press strives to produce its books using methods and materials in an environmentally sensitive manner. We favor working with manufacturers that practice sustainable management of all natural resources, produce paper using recycled stock, and manage forests with the best possible practices for people, biodiversity, and sustainability. The press is a member of the Green Press Initiative, a nonprofit program dedicated to supporting publishers in their efforts to reduce their impacts on endangered forests, climate change, and forest-dependent communities.

The paper used in this publication meets the minimum requirements of the American National Standard for Information Sciences—Permanence of Paper for Printed Library Materials, ANSI 39.48–1992.

CIP data on file at the Library of Congress
29 28 27 26 25 | 5 4 3 2 1

What Does Literature Have to Do with Democracy?

In Zadie Smith's short story "The Waiter's Wife" (1999), three women are sitting on a park bench in 1970s London: Clara Jones, of Jamaican ancestry, pictured by Smith as "a black girl with a winning smile"; Alsana Iqbal, a recently arrived immigrant from Bangladesh; and Neena, Alsana's niece. Clara and Alsana are both pregnant. Clara is expecting a girl and Alsana twin boys. Clara and Alsana have gotten to know each other through their husbands, longtime friends who served together in World War II.

Alsana calls Neena "Niece-of-Shame" because she objects so strongly to Neena's westernized political and cultural opinions, which reflect her experience as a university student. As the women talk and eat, Alsana and her niece quarrel early and often, with Neena provoking Alsana by belittling her as a "little submissive Indian woman" much too subservient to her husband. "It's 1975," Neena scolds Alsana. "You can't conduct relationships like that any more. It's not like back home. There has to be communication between men and women in the West, they've got to listen to each other. . . ." Their conflict escalates when Neena brings up what especially bothers her about Alsana: her arranged marriage ("How could you bear to marry someone you didn't know from Adam?"). An infuriated Alsana defends her marriage as "by far the easier option," but that doesn't stop Neena. Things get even more tense when Neena goes on to lament that Alsana is expecting boys: "I mean, I just think men have caused enough chaos this century. There's enough bloody men in the world. If

I knew I was going to have a boy . . . I'd have to seriously consider abortion."

Alsana is outraged, to put it mildly. She "screams, claps her hands over one of her own ears and one of Clara's" and almost chokes on what she's eating. Clara, who has been quietly listening, finds Neena's comment hysterically funny, perhaps because she knows it's the kind of politically progressive remark that will upend Alsana. Clara has been secretly reading such recently published feminist books as *The Female Eunuch; Sex, Race and Class;* and *Fear of Flying*, all under the covert guidance of Neena, who is trying to rid Clara of her "false consciousness." At this point in the scene, the two pregnant women are beside themselves but for different reasons: one bent over in laughter, "the other in horror and near asphyxiation."

What might have been an enjoyable, relaxing social gathering collapses into angry arguing, triggered by deep disagreement over divisive political and cultural issues. It's a scene that should feel familiar to today's readers, who might have experienced something similar in our own fiercely polarized society: a family Thanksgiving coming apart when someone praises or attacks a political figure, a dispute between patrons of a gym when someone switches the television set to Fox News or MSNBC. Even the specific issues intensifying the argument between Alsana and Neena seem current: the claims of cultural identity, the role of gender, the morality of abortion, the impact of a university education, the weaponization of religion (Alsana pictures her niece burning in hell and thanks Allah for arranging it that way).

The broader social context of the scene also anticipates our own historical moment. Smith describes 1970s London as reeling from accelerated social change precipitated by increased immigration, changing gender roles, challenges to England's standing in the world, and other forces. Some, like Neena, embrace these changes. Others resist them, sometimes violently. Smith's story is punctuated by white-supremacist gangs breaking "basement windows with their steel-capped boots" and threatening people of color. Above all, the sudden quarreling in this scene foreshadows the pessimistic feeling of many people today that sharp political differences are not only unresolvable; they are also inescapable, like a spreading wildfire burning out of control. These deep differences permeate everyday life, igniting fierce clashes without any respite. Not even an afternoon in a park is exempt.

Our experience with comparable clashes might lead us to expect the women, sooner or later, to storm off in anger, to escalate the personal insults they aim at each other, or maybe even to resort to some kind of violence. But something else happens in Smith's story. Hearing all the commotion, Sol Jozefowicz, the park keeper, approaches the women and asks if everything is okay. He specifically asks Clara if she is sure she's all right. Smith describes Clara as being unable to "work out, at this moment, whether she is crying or laughing; the two states suddenly seem only a stone's throw from each other." The disagreement she's witnessing is acquiring a life of its own. It seems so tumultuous and open-ended, so unnecessary and yet so inevitable, it could at any moment dissolve in laughter or inspire even worse fighting.

After some effort, Clara finally gathers herself enough to tell the park keeper, "I'm fine, fine. Sorry to have worried you, Mr. Jozefowicz. Really, I'm fine," to which Alsana responds, still on the attack, "I do not see what so very funny-funny. The murder of the innocents"—her understanding of abortion—"is this funny?" "'Not in my experience,'" Sol replies, "in the collected manner in which he says everything, passing his handkerchief to Clara." Smith beautifully describes the impact of this understated comment and courteous gesture: "It strikes all three women—the way history will: embarrassingly, without warning, like a blush—what the park keeper's experience might have been. They fall silent." Imagining the park keeper's experience as an eastern European Jew jolts the three women. Exposure to his perspective prompts them to realize that because of his history, he might hear "the murder of the innocents" as a description of something other than abortion. Awareness of this other point of view doesn't stop their disagreement, but it does lower the temperature of their quarrel. If the same phrase can have different meanings to different people, maybe what the women see as a clear-cut issue can also allow multiple legitimate points of view. While Neena and Alsana continue to disagree about abortion and other issues, appreciating that others might see things differently tempers their single-minded advocacy. Instead of consigning the other person to hell or false consciousness, they become more willing to share the world with each other even as they disagree.

Here is how Smith describes what happens. Once the park keeper leaves, Neena says to Alsana, "OK, Aunty Alsi. I apologize. I apologize.... What more do you want?" When Alsana replies, Smith hears "her voice losing the fight, becoming vulnerable," as she acknowledges that far from being certain about everything, Alsana longs for "the whole bloody universe [to be] made clear—in a little nutshell. I cannot understand a thing any more." Her self-righteousness and certainty dissolve into self-doubt and hesitation as she concedes that Neena may be right about many things and perhaps sees the truth "better than I." "What do I know," Alsana confesses, "a barefoot country girl who never went to the universities . . ." "Feeling bad," her niece responds, "you know I didn't mean it like that." Alsana and Neena still disagree but in a softer, more temperate way, restrained by their newly acknowledged humility and the importance they attach to retaining their relationship. Attacking each other gives way to apologizing, openly needing the other, their voices "losing the fight" that threatened to pull them apart.

I see this scene as a parable for what sustains vibrant democracies, which is not eliminating disagreement but making it more constructive, by which I mean more like the give-and-take that characterizes interactions between friends than a fight-to-the-finish battle between diehard enemies. In what follows, I propose that reading and discussing works of literature can strengthen the relationships that heathy disagreement—and functioning democracies—depend on. The long-term impact of engaging with works of literature resembles what happens to Smith's characters after they absorb the park keeper's history: it slows down their rush to demonize one another, to defeat or silence the person they are disagreeing with, to retaliate and have the last word, to break off ties instead of repairing them. Before exploring how the study of literature can strengthen democracies in these ways, I need first to look more closely at why unchecked polarization threatens them.

How Democracies Die

In 1998 Hugo Chávez was first elected president of Venezuela. Over the next several years he proceeded to do everything he could to consolidate his power, including restricting the right to vote, arresting or exiling his political opponents, attacking the press and closing a major television station that dared to criticize him, and packing the courts to make sure his retrenchment of democracy could not be contested on legal grounds. In other countries as well—Hungary is one of several examples—elected leaders have similarly subverted democracy from within. It's become a familiar pattern: a democratic form of government gives way to a more authoritarian system, not overnight because a coup dramatically seizes power, but slowly, almost imperceptibly, one withdrawal of rights at a time. In these countries, autocratic leaders typically accelerate this erosion of democracy. By "autocratic leaders," I mean leaders who seek total control and unchecked power. These leaders present themselves as outsiders or populist representatives of "the people," and they promise to save the country by declaring war on the enemies that are supposedly destroying it. In all these instances, a democracy declines gradually, then suddenly, and you're in a different world.

Steven Levitsky and Daniel Ziblatt of Harvard University are two scholars who have studied this pattern. Until recently, their research concentrated on countries in Latin America and Europe. Their work shifted focus when they collaborated on a 2018 book, *How Democracies Die*. Instead of revisiting the countries they had been studying, they presented a new case study of a democracy they thought was now at risk: the United States.

How Democracies Die identifies several indicators for when a democracy might be in trouble—indicators that, in democracies which devolve into autocracies, citizens ignore or minimize until it is too late. These warning signs include when some political leaders and their followers reject the democratic rules of the game, for example by undermining the legitimacy of elections and refusing to accept credible electoral results. Another sign is when these leaders and their followers deny the legitimacy of their political opponents, typically by claiming that they constitute threats to national security or to the prevailing way of life. Still another is when they tolerate or encourage violence, either by engaging in violent rhetoric or by maintaining ties to paramilitary organizations committed to using force. This proclivity to violence accompanies a willingness to restrict individual rights and curtail free expression in the press, in schools and universities, and in literature and the arts.

In *How Democracies Die*, Levitsky and Ziblatt argue that democracies work best and survive longer when unwritten norms, or what they call "soft guardrails," reinforce democratic institutions and keep autocratic tendencies in check. They highlight two norms especially important to democracies: mutual toleration, which motivates competing political parties to accept one another as legitimate rivals, and forbearance, which encourages elected leaders to regard the holding of political office as a temporary privilege, not an opportunity to seize power once and for all and to eliminate their political rivals, as Chávez tried to do. By demonstrating forbearance—that is, by showing restraint in how they use their authority—elected officials acknowledge that they are subject to checks and balances, including a free press, the rule of law, an independent judiciary, and the will of the majority, which elections determine.

I want to look more closely at the assumption that there are unwritten norms or soft guardrails that safeguard a democracy. I focus on these underlying norms not only because of their importance to democracy but because, in my view, the humanities—specifically, the study of literature—can play a crucial role at this level. For Levitsky and Ziblatt, forbearance and mutual tolerance are two of the uncodified rules democratic leaders acknowledge. Other writers on democracy have argued that to be effective, these rules need to find reinforcement at a more basic level in the values and relationships that shape everyday interactions among citizens. In what is still one of the most important books on democracy, Alexis de Tocqueville's two-volume *Democracy in America*, published in 1835 and 1840, Tocqueville discusses the attitudes toward one another that citizens must cultivate in their daily lives to sustain democratic institutions. He calls these attitudes "habits of the heart," a phrase I'll also be using.

In healthy democracies, according to Tocqueville, citizens develop these habits of the heart in their daily life with one another in neighborhoods, workplaces, schools and universities, volunteer organizations, and other places where they get together every day. Over time, these everyday interactions influence political behavior. By political behavior, I mean, for example, how members of city councils, legislatures, or school boards do their work together, how candidates for office regard their opponents and treat journalists, how citizens in line to vote at a polling place treat one another and the volunteer workers supervising an election, how they participate in public meetings. In healthy democracies, mutually respectful everyday interactions soften political differences by putting them in the context of deeper social connections. Our ties to one another help us take seriously our ongoing political disagreements without, however, allowing them to tear us apart.

A current writer indebted to Tocqueville is the political theorist Danielle Allen. In her 2004 book *Talking to Strangers: Anxieties of Citizenship since* Brown v. Board of Education, Allen characterizes the habits of the heart essential to democracy as "practices of political friendship." Allen's academic area of specialization is the literature of ancient Greece and Rome. She takes the phrase "practices of political friendship" from Aristotle's writings on rhetoric and politics. By this phrase, she means how friends work out their differences in everyday life, how they stay friends while disagreeing and sometimes getting frustrated with one another. The Zadie Smith story I began with shows friendship in action, as the three women work through their differences, learning how to assert these differences without letting them ruin their relationship. The practices that shore up friendship include how friends demonstrate to one another their willingness to share power and to take turns exercising control; how they make sure that concessions even out over time, as opposed to one party always giving in to the other; how they trust that their friend will reciprocate their willingness to compromise, not take advantage of it; how they're willing apologize to one another when they think they've gone too far. The title of Allen's book,

Talking to Strangers, recalls her mother's advice when she was growing up, which was "don't talk to strangers." But in everyday life we interact with strangers all the time. Allen is urging us to interact with strangers as if they were our friends—not to reserve the practices of friendship only for the people we know or agree with, but to let these practices extend to others as well.

Allen argues that in healthy democracies, these everyday practices of friendship put pressure on how we navigate our inevitable political differences:

> Political order is secured not only by institutions, but also by "deep rules" that prescribe specific interactions among citizens in public spaces; citizens enact what they are to each other not only in assemblies, where they make decisions about their mutually intertwined fates, but also when, as strangers, they speak to one another, or don't, or otherwise respond to each other's presence.

Among the practices of friendship that Allen values, mutual trust is especially important to democracies. As she puts it,

> Trust is not something that politicians alone can create. It grows only among citizens as they rub shoulders in daily life—in supermarkets, at movie theaters, on buses, at amusement parks, and in airports—and wherever they participate in maintaining an institution, whether a school, a church, or a business.

Trust among citizens is so important to Allen because she focuses in her book on the ferocious backlash unleashed by the Supreme Court's 1954 *Brown v. Board of Education* decision to end segregation in public schools. Allen is deeply disturbed by the scene of a young Black woman, Elizabeth Eckford, trying in 1957 to attend an all-white high school in Little Rock, Arkansas, as a unanimous Supreme Court decision authorized her to do. Angry adults blocked Elizabeth's way, screaming and cursing at her, brandishing signs reading "Stop the Race Mixing March of the Anti-Christ" and other vitriolic slogans. For Allen, this backlash shows how even laws and unanimous court decisions need broader cultural support to become effective. The backlash also illustrates for Allen the corrosive impact of racism on democracy. Racism is unequivocally incompatible with democracy and disqualifying in a political leader because it shatters every practice of political friendship democracies depend on. The hatred unleashed by racism inspires endlessly looking for new targets to attack and exclude.

Nothing could be more antithetical to a healthy democracy than the ugliness that rained down on Elizabeth Eckford. As I have been emphasizing, healthy democracies thrive on constructive disagreement; they collapse when that disagreement devolves into violent attacks aimed at silencing, humiliating, and shutting out others.

HOW BOOKS CAN SAVE DEMOCRACY

When I imagine a vibrant democracy, I picture individuals and groups sharing the world with people who differ from them, creating a diverse community together, talking with one another and working things out on school boards, city councils, and in many other settings, benefiting from exchanges that encourage free expression, independent thinking, and healthy questioning. Robust democracies feed off the proliferation of different points of view and the productive debates that can result when these views engage with one another.

When I talk about working things out with others and constructively resolving disputes, I do not mean arriving at some fixed consensus that moves us to give up our differences. I mean arriving at decisions and courses of action amid continuing conflict, agreeing on some points while still disagreeing on others, which is what happens in functioning democracies when, after much debate, split juries reach a verdict, divided legislatures pass laws, and closely contested elections conclude with one candidate conceding victory to another. In all these scenarios, no agreement or outcome ever decides things once and for all. There are always ambiguities, unresolved issues, and lingering differences of opinion that can flare up later and undo what has been accomplished. But the experience of constructively dealing with differences gives people the confidence that they can work their way through future conflicts when they arise, as they inevitably will. The goal of conflict resolution in a democracy, in other words, is to find ways of navigating our ongoing differences with others, not wishing these differences away. We can agree to disagree on some issues while concurring on others.

Because democracies thrive on generating different points of view, democratic leaders honor the need to live with their opponents even after defeating them. Out of respect for maintaining an ongoing relationship with their adversaries, these leaders are generous, not vindictive. They don't gloat. When things go well for them, they refrain from trying to turn their electoral success into an opportunity to squelch their rivals once and for all. When things don't go so well, these leaders acknowledge their opponents as legitimate participants in the political process entitled to win, not treasonable foes or intolerable threats.

One such democratic leader was Nelson Mandela, who in many ways exemplifies the attitudes toward others that democracies depend on. In his book *Bargaining with the Devil: When to Negotiate, When to Fight*, Robert Mnookin, former chair of the Program on Negotiation at Harvard Law School, points out that when Mandela was elected president of South Africa, he had every reason in the world not to negotiate with his political opponents. These reasons included twenty-three years of unjust imprisonment, compounded by the lack of any personal connection to President F. W. de Klerk, head of the opposition National Party, which had presided over apartheid. Mandela also faced pressure from some of his own followers, who urged him to retaliate and strike back, even violently, at their adversaries now that they had the chance. Mandela resisted this pressure and his own deep reservations about de Klerk, passing up opportunities for retribution and revenge even when others were encouraging him to exploit them. Mnookin calls Mandela one of the best negotiators of the twentieth century because in negotiating with his adversaries and his own allies, he struck the right balance between openness to other points of view and the principled assertion of his own. As Mnookin concludes,

> Mandela was a negotiator to whom one could make concessions and yet maintain one's self-respect. Mandela worked hard to establish and maintain a personal, human connection with Afrikaner leaders whose life experiences and attitudes were radically different from his own. These leaders came to see that Mandela really believed in racial reconciliation. They saw that his vision for South Africa included them.

Mandela was a great negotiator, not because he always won, but because he defused the life-or-death consequences others attached to winning and losing. He aimed not at seizing absolute power for himself or his side but at repairing a war-torn country and launching a new democracy. He exemplified the habits of the heart upon which the future health of that democracy would depend.

Mandela especially excelled at two core democratic values. The first is receptivity to compromise, which I characterize as the willingness to modify one's own position to accommodate the interests of others, sometimes by crediting them with better ideas (as Alsana does when she admits her niece might be right about some things), sometimes by making concessions because others attach importance to the points in question and deserve a chance to leave their mark on an agreement. Compromise is not appeasement or going along to get along while sacrificing one's integrity in the process. Instead of unilaterally giving in, compromise in a democracy emerges from the give-and-take of dialogue, from asserting one's convictions and listening to opposing views.

The philosopher Avishai Margalit writes that compromise "breathes life into democracy." Amy Gutman and Dennis Thompson similarly call compromise "the artistry of democracy" and suggest that in a democracy, "there is no escape from compromise" because even if one side controls a legislative body or court, members will still have to work through their internal differences. The push and pull of differences in a democracy can be so strong that sometimes not even calls for party unity and loyalty can curtail them. At bottom, receptivity to compromise registers a willingness to share the world: to live with one's adversaries and to keep people talking to one other, whether they are getting their way on a particular issue or losing out.

The second building block of democracy that Mandela embraced is the readiness to ask for and extend forgiveness, as the characters in Smith's story do when they begin repairing their fraying relationship. Here I'm describing a frame of mind that keeps conflicts from needlessly escalating. It's the willingness of people in a disagreement to be patient with one another, to let some things go, and to keep what may be lower-level annoyances and irritations from mushrooming into full-blown tensions. This openness to forgiveness is the opposite of an accusatory frame of mind that is always on guard, seeing every dispute as a power struggle and constantly looking out for reasons to counterattack and gain the upper hand against implacable adversaries. Shakespeare captures this vindictive frame of mind in the character of Malvolio in his play *Twelfth Night*. Toward the end of the play, Malvolio storms offstage, determined to get revenge on some people who have played a joke on him. Before he leaves, one character tells him, "Oh, you are sick of self-love, Malvolio, and taste with a distempered appetite. To be generous, guiltless and of free disposition, is to take those things for bird-bolts that you deem cannon-bullets."

Much as a generous, free disposition can keep molehills from mushrooming into mountains, being willing to extend and seek forgiveness can defang even the most intense conflicts once they are underway. Mandela knew that holding a grudge, reliving past disputes, and single-mindedly pursuing retribution prolong conflict and make it even worse. As the philosopher Hannah Arendt observed, being open to forgiveness frees both sides in a conflict from "the predicament of irreversibility," or being defined once and for all by something done or said in the past. As Arendt goes on to say, "without being forgiven, released from the consequences of what we have done, our capacity to act would . . . be confined to one single deed from which we would never recover." Allowing for the possibility of forgiveness tempers moral judgment but does not eliminate it. It provides opportunities for earning another chance, trying again, and releasing the goodwill that riveting attention on the past bottles up. Thinking of how being willing to forgive can allow disputants to move on, Archbishop Desmond Tutu went so far as to entitle a book *No Future without Forgiveness*.

It is striking how at critical moments in democracies, farsighted leaders invoke forgiveness as a way forward from civil strife. I have in mind Abraham Lincoln's second inaugural address in 1865. With the end of the Civil War in sight, Lincoln spoke of "malice toward none" and "charity for all" as he pledged "to finish the work we are in to bind up the nation's wounds." In a similar spirit, the South African parliament established the Truth and Reconciliation Commission in April 1994, shortly after the abolition of apartheid and the election of Mandela. Many South Africans understood that Mandela's election, while a historic step forward, needed additional support for a new democracy to take root and gain strength. The country remained deeply divided, and many feared that a civil war spawned by apartheid's brutal past could undermine the fragile, emerging democratic order. Just as one Supreme Court decision could not end racism and segregation in the

United States, one election could not by itself overcome a legacy of injustice, oppression, and exploitation and magically put in its place a culture of respect for equality and universal human rights. But the fledgling South African democracy was not going to get the traction it needed by simply punishing white Afrikaners for their unquestionably horrible offenses. The Truth and Reconciliation Commission gave the victims of apartheid the opportunity to tell their stories and thereby invite public acknowledgment of the injustice they experienced. The commission also offered the possibility of amnesty for those individuals who publicly took responsibility for the harm they had done and expressed their determination to treat all citizens with respect in the future. Although the process wasn't perfect, it did help unify the country and strengthen confidence in peacefully resolving ongoing internal conflicts—a confidence that is crucial to sustaining democracies.

Finally, Mandela exemplified one other central democratic value: empathy, by which I mean the capacity to understand the feelings of another, in Mandela's case even someone as distant and unsympathetic as de Klerk. In practice, seeing the world through the eyes of others credits them with the same humanity we claim for ourselves: the same capacity for hope, love, fear, and grief that informs our own lives and gives us the right to expect consideration from others. Mandela's willingness to establish a personal connection with his adversaries bolstered his ability to compromise with them and allow them a chance to move with him beyond the past. By strengthening his relationships with Afrikaner leaders, Mandela backed up his commitment to include them in the new society taking shape. He gave them reasons to trust that his vision of South Africa included them.

In dysfunctional or faltering democracies, the values I have been attributing to Mandela collapse into their opposites. Empathy gives way to bitter polarization and dehumanization, compromise to unyielding opposition, and forgiveness to an unrelenting quest for retribution.

A perpetual fight to the finish results when despising one's adversaries drives decisions and commitments. I am for *x* because the opponents I despise are against it, and I will do everything I can to defeat what I see as their threat to who I am and what I value. I can't imagine talking with these adversaries, let alone working things out with them. The issue triggering unbounded conflict between bitter enemies can be almost anything, from climate change and public health policies to the choice of a carryout. The constructive debates that democracies depend on devolve into shouting matches or vicious attacks that disputants can imagine ending only when their side wipes out the other.

Like the people cursing Elizabeth Eckford, citizens who have lost faith in dialogue, elections, and persuasion gravitate toward undemocratic ways of achieving their political goals, including bullying, intimidation, violence, and in some cases support for authoritarian leaders who promise to protect their supporters from their despicable enemies and to get things done on their behalf. The autocratic boast "I alone can fix it" gains support when people lose confidence in working out their differences with others. In dysfunctional democracies, in short, opportunities for disagreement multiply while trust in peacefully resolving conflict declines. It is a terrible combination. In these backsliding democracies, instead of everyday life tempering political differences (Tocqueville's ideal), toxic political divisions seep into everyday life, turning even friends and family members into strangers and adversaries. There's no escaping political strife, no respite from all the fighting. The habits of the heart that sustain democracy can't find a foothold anywhere, not even in an everyday lunch in a park. We end up dreading family gatherings instead of looking forward to them.

Philip Roth memorably captures this picture of a democracy in trouble in his 2004 novel *The Plot against America*, which imagines a fictional Charles Lindbergh getting elected president of the United States in 1940 on the eve of World War II on a frankly anti-Semitic, pro-Nazi platform. At one point a young character in a Jewish family overhears his older brother, who supports Lindbergh, angrily arguing about politics with their mother. When the mother snaps at her son, "You don't know what you're talking about!" the son replies, "But you won't listen. If it wasn't for President Lindbergh . . ." We don't hear his defense of Lindbergh because Roth shifts our attention to his younger brother saying to himself, "That name again!" The younger brother is sick of hearing about Lindbergh, thinking about him, worrying about what he'll do next, listening to others arguing endlessly about him. The dejected younger brother thinks, "I would rather have heard a bomb go off than to have to hear one more time the name that was tormenting us all." But he can neither escape talking about Lindbergh nor stop the president from permeating every corner of his life, even his home.

Lindbergh is here achieving a key goal of all autocratic leaders, which is to dominate every conversation, monopolize attention, and keep people constantly angry, fearful, and on edge. By saturating everyday life with his presence, Lindbergh creates the feeling among his followers that he is as inescapable as the air they breathe, and as necessary. These followers begin to feel that their lives are inextricably bound up with the leader, their future dependent on his, no matter what he says or does. Lindbergh's primary tactic is the familiar authoritarian one of identifying and vilifying a marginalized group (in this case, Jews) and pledging to protect his followers against that group's supposed threat to their lives. Like other autocratic leaders, Lindbergh asserts he alone can defeat these enemies. His claim of indispensability reinforces Allen's point about how racism and authoritarianism are intertwined. Authoritarian leaders thrive on pitting "the real people" against "them," where "them" expands to include whichever group these leaders can demonize to intensify the unconditional loyalty they seek. The hatred unleashed by racism metastasizes and eases the way toward dehumanizing these other groups.

When individuals or groups come to think of others as mortal enemies out to destroy their way of life, dialogue with these adversaries seems futile, even dangerous. Withdrawing or violently striking back makes more sense. We get talk of a civil war and calls for action against irredeemable enemies, as when Ryan Walters, state superintendent of Oklahoma's State Board of Education, recently defended his state's restrictive gender policies in the wake of the death of a sixteen-year-old nonbinary student after an altercation in a high school girls' bathroom: "I really see there's a civil war going on, where the left is really fighting for the soul of our country," he said. "They are undermining the very principles that made this country great, our Judeo-Christian values and our traditions in this country."

A growing number of people in contemporary America are taking the next step and translating into action what they think "fighting for the soul of our country" means. It doesn't mean engaging in a debate. Here is a recent example of what I mean. At the United States Capitol on January 6, 2021, a truck driver assaulted a police officer with a flagpole. He was sentenced in the summer of 2023 to fifty-two months in federal prison. He was captured on video furiously beating the officer who was lying face down overwhelmed by a mob of other rioters with no means of defending himself. The assailant was one of nine men charged with assaulting the officer and two of his colleagues. After this vicious attack, the assailant was caught on video pointing at the Capitol and declaring: "Everybody in there is a disgrace. That entire building is filled with treasonous traitors. Death is the only remedy for what's in that building." He went on to say that for "every single one of those Capitol law enforcement officers, death is the remedy. That is the only remedy they get." Tragically, you can find comparable blanket dismissals of others repeated by the gunman who killed eleven people and wounded six at a Pittsburgh synagogue in 2018 or the man who shot and killed ten Black people at a Buffalo supermarket in 2022 or the El Paso man who in 2019 killed twenty people and injured more than two dozen others in response to "the Hispanic invasion of Texas." It's a long list.

With these examples, and many more I could cite, we're a far cry from the constructive disagreement that characterizes healthy democracies, which is one reason why Levitsky and Ziblatt and others worry that democracy may be dying in America. I sense in my students at Trinity University, all of them undergraduates around eighteen to twenty-one years old, deep skepticism about the possibility of addressing disagreements through dialogue with people who hold different points of view. When I think of the world my students have grown up in, I am not surprised by their skepticism. They are pessimistic about resolving differences through discussion, not because they embrace antidemocratic values but because wherever they look—the media, the courts, Congress and state legislatures, campaign debates, churches and synagogues, school boards—they see disagreement:

- » triggering paralysis and inaction on the most urgent causes, including racial justice, gun control, public health safety measures, and climate change
- » unleashing purveyors of disinformation, unconstrained conspiracy theorists, and angry fomenters of chaos, all of them acting on Steve Bannon's advice to "flood the zone with shit," whether the zone is a school board meeting or neighborhood gathering, the topic vaccines and masks, the K–12 curriculum, or the legitimacy of a presidential election
- » spurring on personal attacks, unchecked bullying, and racist, misogynistic assaults aimed at silencing less powerful voices, particularly on social media sites.

For my students, disagreement in action is not a Nelson Mandela cultivating an emerging democracy by negotiating with critics on his left and on his right. Instead, disagreement in action conjures up rioters like the one I mentioned earlier, storming the nation's capitol to contest a presidential election; a congressman sharing an anime video starring himself killing a young female member of the other party; a town hall meeting, as described by *Politico*, resembling a riot, with "screaming constituents, protesters dragged out by the cops, congressmen fearful for their safety." The damage to democracy done by these scenes is immense. Autocratic leaders want to incapacitate citizens from working out things on their own, which is why these leaders sow the confusion, fear, and anger these scenes represent. These feelings perpetuate powerlessness, which in turn encourages resorting to force and siding with strong-armed leaders who pledge to resolve intractable disputes in favor of their followers.

I share my students' doubts about the supposed benefits disagreement currently brings to our world. I also share their weariness with all the fighting, their hopelessness when partisan wrangling stalls yet another urgently needed legislative proposal. Like the young boy in *The Plot against America,* many of the people I encounter in my classes and daily life are sick of the endless arguing that they see tearing apart neighborhoods, families, and many institutions. Former U.S. Ambassador to the United Nations Nikki Haley was onto something when she remarked during the 2024 Republican presidential primary, "We got to stop where we are hating people because they're on the other side. We got to stop with all this anger and division that's happening around our country." With young people in mind, she went on to say, "They can't live like that. It is not right." Along with everything else on their minds as they are thinking about their futures, "all they feel is anger and chaos."

Haley's comment triggered this predictable reaction from her opponent's campaign: "This is what weak babies say when they don't have enough fortitude to run INTO the fire to fight for what's right." This is a PG-rated version of the vitriolic online abuse aimed Haley's way: the taunts, threats, insults, and smears targeting her gender, her ethnic background, her citizenship, and family. With this kind of response guaranteed, disenchantment with destructive conflict risks turning into withdrawal, or fleeing from all the fighting, which is of course exactly what these attacks seek.

I am encouraged, however, by the many attempts springing up in our society to redeem disagreement and restore faith in its constructive potential, which are essential to democracy. These efforts include recent initiatives in dispute resolution that seek to help people in a conflict understand their differences instead of going to war over them. In a recent essay, "Living with No: Polarization and Transformative Dialogue" (2018), three experienced mediators cite their encouraging experiences facilitating community dialogues where no decisions are at stake. These face-to-face encounters enable participants with starkly opposing points of view to find constructive ways of expressing their positions while listening to others. Participants begin learning to live with differences instead of regarding them as insuperable barriers to cooperation. As Peter T. Coleman concludes in *The Way Out: How to Overcome Toxic Polarization* (2021), mediators in our polarized culture are learning to *"start small"* and "to play the *long game*" by creating "bubbles of functionality in seas of hate and dysfunction," which over time may inspire constructive approaches to conflict when decisions are at stake.

Along similar lines, new centers, courses, and programs promoting healthy dialogue are appearing on university campuses across the country. The Kellogg School of Management at Northwestern University, for example, recently launched a Center for Enlightened Disagreement dedicated to identifying best practices and training students and leaders "on how to engage across differences and harness the power of diverse perspectives." In announcing the center, Kellogg School dean Francesca Cornelli emphasized the center's commitment "to addressing the growing barriers to discourse that hinder our progress as a society, not by seeking to eliminate disagreement but by embracing it as a virtue." "Now is the time to expand this work," Dean Cornelli concluded, "which has never been more essential."

Along similar lines, numerous commissions and study groups are developing proposals for reforming institutions and overhauling laws to counter toxic polarization. In 2020 the American Academy of Arts and Sciences, to cite only one example, established a Commission on the Practice of Democratic Citizenship (Danielle Allen served as one of the co-chairs). Its June 2020 report—*Our Common Purpose: Reinventing American Democracy for the 21st Century*—outlines several measures that would counter the "disruptive media and information environment, outdated political institutions, economic and social inequality," and other forces fueling destructive conflict. These measures include increasing the size of the House of Representatives, setting up multimember districts designed by independent citizen redistricting commissions, instituting ranked-choice voting, eradicating the filibuster in the Senate, establishing same-day voter registration, and creating staggered eighteen-year terms for Supreme Court justices. If implemented, these measures and others would carry out the report's reminder that "democracy, when it works, is not a battle whose purpose is annihilation of the enemy; it is, if it works, a game of infinite repeat play that includes ever-more participants."

How Books Can Strengthen Democracy

"If implemented," of course, is the key. It is easy to be cynical about these efforts and doubt their chances of success against the powerful forces arrayed against them. No one is promising a quick fix to the challenges facing American democracy. But advocates for institutional change working in tandem with teachers, writers, artists, and other cultural leaders can, over time, be a powerful combination in rebuilding confidence that a multiracial, pluralistic democracy can work instead of disintegrating into civil war. So many things can make a democracy vulnerable and need our attention. But nurturing the underlying relationships, values, and attitudes that sustain democracies plays an essential role in shoring up the conditions that sustain institutional change, which is why I turn now to one overlooked resource for rehabilitating American democracy: the humanities, more specifically, the study of literature.

In her 2023 book *Justice by Means of Democracy*, Danielle Allen notes some startling patterns in how the humanities and the STEM disciplines (science, technology, engineering, and mathematics) prepare students for engagement in political life. According to data gathered by the United States Department of Education, among 2008 college graduates, 92.8 percent of humanities majors have voted at least once since leaving their universities, versus 83.5 percent of STEM majors. Within ten years after graduation, 44.1 percent of 1993 humanities graduates had written to public officials, versus 30.1 percent of STEM majors. In addition, according to a 2005 study by political scientist Sunshine Hillygus, differences in political engagement begin to take shape in precollege education. High verbal scores on the SAT correlate with increased likelihood of political participation, while high math scores on the SAT correlate with decreased likelihood of participation. Allen is careful to say that a healthy democratic society needs both the STEM fields and the humanities in education at every level, which is my position, too. But there is something about the humanities that especially prepares young people for democratic citizenship. The study of literature clarifies what that is.

Important works of literature have always addressed the urgent political issues of their times. Sometimes these literary works have had an immediate, measurable impact. A classic example in American literature is Upton Sinclair's 1905 novel *The Jungle*, an exposé of the meatpacking industry in Chicago that led to important sanitation reforms, including the 1906 Meat Inspection Act. Tackling current issues remains one way works of literature can influence society.

I am interested here, however, in works of literature that take up more personal or general experiences, such as growing up, falling in or out of love, becoming a parent, choosing a vocation, and grieving the death of someone you love. These works play an especially important role in strengthening the values and relationships that sustain healthy democracies.

Before developing this point, I want to acknowledge that studying literature is valuable but not omnipotent. Its impact requires reinforcement from supportive schools and universities, thoughtful political leaders, and many other forces. Even under the best of circumstances, the social influence of literary study is not automatic or immediate but gradual and cumulative. Its benefits are more like those of everyday physical exercise than dramatic life-saving surgery. As the writer Elaine Scarry has said, "It's not that I read [a work of literature] and then go out and care about more people." Nevertheless, by fostering over time what Scarry calls "a greater pliancy of thinking, a greater openness to the concerns of others," works of literature nurture attitudes toward others crucial to democracy.

Empathy is another word for "openness to the concerns of others." Linking literature to empathy gets support from many quarters. Psychologists, for example, have conducted empirical studies demonstrating that reading literature strengthens what they call "theory of mind" or the capacity to discern and "mirror" how others are feeling: for example, wincing when someone else gets hurt, feeling sad when another person is grieving, or getting anxious when someone is about to do something we know they're nervous about. These psychological studies document that reading literature can sharpen responsiveness to what others may be feeling.

In addition to psychologists, historians have argued that works of literature help democratize societies by opening the eyes of readers to the lives of people these readers would otherwise never know. Scarry cites the historian Lynn Hunt, who traces the eighteenth-century development of human rights in part to people reading some of the best-selling novels of the day, such as Samuel Richardson's *Clarissa*, and "thereby entering imaginatively into the lives of other people, including those without social power: women, servants, and children." Scarry adds that when as readers we follow a dialogue between two characters—say, an exchange between two family members who find themselves at odds on a particular point like the mother and son in Roth's novel—we tap into what Scarry calls the "capacity of literature to exercise and reinforce our recognition that there are other points of view in the world, and to make this recognition a powerful mental habit." Such recognition dawns on the quarreling characters in Smith's short story when they hear another interpretation of a phrase they've been using. When I liken studying literature to everyday physical exercise, this is the capacity we're exercising: the capacity to see things from other points of view, which a spirited dialogue between characters can bring to light.

I am struck by how many novelists, playwrights, and poets describe their work as strengthening connections with others. As the

English poet Percy Bysshe Shelley wrote in his *Defence of Poetry*, "The great secret of morals is love, a going out of our own nature, and an identification of ourselves with the beautiful which exists in thought, action, or person not our own. A man, to be greatly good, must imagine intensely and comprehensively; he must put himself in the place of another and of many others; the pains and pleasures of his species must become his own. The great instrument of moral good is the imagination and poetry administers to the effect by acting upon the cause." Sometimes even the titles of works of literature suggest how these works aim at deepening insight into others, particularly people the authors assume their readers overlook. I'm thinking here, for example, of the African American writer Ralph Ellison's 1952 novel *Invisible Man* and Cristina Henríquez's 2014 novel *The Book of Unknown Americans*, which focuses on the experience of Panamanian and Mexican immigrants to the United States, experiences that might remain unknown to some readers without fiction bringing them to light.

Finally, some of the most compelling arguments for aligning literature with empathy come from philosophers interested in ethics or, more specifically, in how individuals arrive at their moral values and act on them. One of these philosophers is Martha Nussbaum. A common philosophical approach to teaching ethics equates morality with arriving at general rules for how we ought to conduct our lives and then using these rules to assess arguments for and against abortion, capital punishment, and other controversial moral issues. While appreciating the insights resulting from this approach, Nussbaum finds in literature a richer account of how in practice we try to live decent lives. Works of literature, unlike abstract philosophical arguments, typically embed our moral exchanges with others in particular relationships and contexts. By moral exchanges, I mean what we do when we apologize to someone, express disappointment or approval, decline or accept a request to do something, among the many other things we do when we interact with others.

Nussbaum argues that leading a moral life requires being attentive to others, or becoming people "on whom nothing is lost" in our dealings with them. Becoming a person "on whom nothing is lost" is also how the American novelist Henry James described the task of the literary artist, leading Nussbaum to conclude that "the work of the moral imagination is in some manner like the creative imagination, especially that of the novelist." What we ought to do in a particular situation, in other words, depends not only on appealing to general rules but on accurately perceiving the people we are interacting with: seeing them in all their complexity, taking in what they are saying or showing to us, and responding to them with imagination and feeling.

A scene from Charles Dickens's 1854 novel *Hard Times* will help me illustrate this point. A father, Mr. Gradgrind, has told his young daughter Louisa that his friend Mr. Bounderby wants to marry her. No reader has ever wanted Louisa to accept this proposal. For many reasons, the vast age difference between Mr. Bounderby and

Louisa being only one of them, this marriage would be a grotesque pairing; calling it cringeworthy barely scratches the surface of all that is wrong with it. The scene starts with Louisa asking her father, "Shall I marry him?" This is a personal and a moral question. She's asking her father's help in figuring out what she should do. Knowing what we as readers know about Louisa and Mr. Bounderby by this point in the novel, I imagine Louisa wondering, "Why I am so repulsed by this offer? Should I be? What do I want for my life? What can I realistically hope for? What am I here for in this world?" These concerns lie beneath what she asks her father. His success at advising his daughter will depend on his sensing what she may be feeling but not saying.

Here is how Dickens describes the exchange between the two:

> "Shall I marry him?" repeated Louisa, with great deliberation.
>
> "Precisely. And it is satisfactory to me, as your father, my dear Louisa, to know that you'd not come to the consideration

of that question with the previous habits of mind, and habits of life, that belong to many young women."

"No, father," she returned, "I do not."

"I now leave you to judge for yourself," said Mr. Gradgrind. "I have stated the case, as such cases are usually stated among practical minds; I have stated it, as the case of your mother and myself was stated in its time. The rest, my dear Louisa, is for you to decide."

From the beginning, she had sat looking at him fixedly. As he now leaned back in his chair, and bent his deep-set eyes upon her in his turn, perhaps he might have seen one wavering moment in her, when she was impelled to throw herself upon his breast, and give him the pent-up confidences of her heart. But, to see it, he must have overleaped at a bound the artificial barriers he had for many years been erecting, between himself and all those subtle essences of humanity which will elude the utmost cunning of algebra until the last trumpet ever to be sounded shall blow even algebra to wreck. The barriers were too many and too high for such a leap. With his unbending, utilitarian, matter-of-fact face, he hardened her again; and the moment shot away into the plumbless depths of the past, to mingle with all the lost opportunities that are drowned there.

Dickens is appalled by Mr. Gradgrind's obtuseness here, his failing to see his daughter longing for some encouragement from him, some invitation or permission for her to reveal what she is really feeling and sharing it with him instead of keeping it pent up in her own heart. I happen to think Mr. Gradgrind loves his daughter; certainly, he thinks he is carrying out his responsibility to her by relaying Mr. Bounderby's proposal and hearing what she has to say. But his obliviousness is a serious moral failing that betrays her and lets her fall into a disastrous marriage that will cause her much pain. Mr. Gradgrind not only doesn't see his daughter's anguish; he's also blind to what he has done in his own life to deaden his responsiveness to her, the barriers he's erected to keep others out, his own family included. He is as clueless about himself as he is about her.

Significantly, Mr. Gradgrind oversees a harshly utilitarian school that Louisa and her brother attend. This school excludes the study of literature, an omission that contributes to Mr. Gradgrind's lack of insight into himself and others. He's a person on whom just about everything is lost, including his own daughter's cry for help. His failure at empathy reminds us how the skills fostered by studying literature—the skills he has let atrophy—can enrich our everyday lives with one another, when we put down our books and resume the unending quest to understand others and ourselves.

Sometimes you don't know what you've got until it's almost gone. Appreciating how works of literature can strengthen insight into others shows why banning books, removing them from classrooms and libraries, is so damaging to a democracy. In my view, the very need to take books from libraries and restrict what students read is a backhanded tribute to the power of literature that I have been describing. For me, it's inspiring that some of the most passionate defenders of reading literature today are what I would call first responders to the censorship efforts underway in several states: I mean K–12 teachers, parents, librarians, and students who testify to what reading literature can do.

Here is one example. In a recent essay, the writer Taylor Brorby recalls growing up in North Dakota as a self-described closeted gay teenager. Brorby discovered a "sanctuary in libraries" that he could find nowhere else: a place where he could, in his words, "find stories that made [him] feel [he] could fit in, not only in North Dakota, but in the wider world," stories by James Baldwin, Truman Capote, and Willa Cather. Later, after he graduated from college and returned home, he would frequent the Bismarck Veterans Memorial Public Library, where stories of LGBTQ people helped him find his way to what he calls "stable ground." He remembers local libraries as places where he was "free to roam, peruse, and free to be [himself], at least privately." He concludes, "I don't know where I would have ended up if I couldn't have read my way out of despair. My heart breaks to think of all the kids now who won't have that option."

I have been describing how reading literature can deepen attentiveness to others. In "The Most Important Writing Exercise I've Ever Assigned," the novelist Rachel Kadish looks at the role of literature from a different angle, namely, from the perspective of aspiring writers. In her creative writing classes, Kadish explores the claim that the moral judgments we make in everyday life resemble the artistic decisions writers make in creating characters and stories. Kadish asks her students to write down a phrase they find abhorrent—something so objectionable that they can't imagine ever saying it. To counter their tendency to censor themselves, she assures them they won't have to show it to anyone. After some hesitation, the students typically comply with her request, but her next prompt is even more unsettling. She asks them to spend ten minutes writing a monologue in the first person spoken by a fictitious character that includes the offensive statement they have just written. Embedding the comment in a specific character's story often puts it in a context that doesn't excuse or justify the comment but allows it to make some sense, at least for this speaker with this history in these circumstances.

The exercise sparks an unexpected moment of empathy, as the students experience something they previously thought impossible: "repugnance for a behavior or worldview coupled with recognition of shared humanity."

In any deep-seated disagreement, disputants can experience what Mnookin calls in *Bargaining with the Devil* the "fear of empathizing." He is quoting a symphony musician embroiled in a bitter labor dispute who found individuals on both sides ambivalent about hearing the other side, lest it make it harder for them to fortify themselves against their adversary. Similarly, Kadish has seen her students, whatever their political views, struggle with this classroom exercise, fearing that any fellow feeling they might develop toward their created characters will disarm their antipathy to the reprehensible views these characters support. Kadish worries that in our current fractious political climate, this classroom exercise has gotten even harder. She suggests that "maybe there are times so contentious or so painful that people simply withdraw to their own silos" and that "a leap into someone else's perspective feels impossible."

I think she's right about this being one of those times. I would add that the willingness to understand someone else's perspective has become more difficult, and the longing to ward off that understanding more appealing, because the range of objectionable statements students can draw on has so dramatically expanded in our toxic political culture. These statements now include not just uninformed or questionable assumptions about a particular issue but also unabashedly racist attacks, misogynistic insults, and cruel misrepresentations, often echoing the rhetoric of major political figures. Nevertheless, I would agree with Kadish that empathizing with others remains "the job of the writer, and there's no point in doing it halfway." Despite the obstacles lined up against it, "good fiction pulls off a magic trick of absurd power: It makes us care," even when we may not want to.

I have been suggesting that the job of the writer as Kadish describes it is also the responsibility of the citizen. Kadish notes how in one of her classes, a pro-choice student came up with a phrase condemning abortion, while across the way a pro-life student created a phrase defending it. Both students then faced the challenge of writing a monologue inviting them to grasp the full complexity of the character whose view repelled them. In both instances, the writing exercise bridged a gap the students thought insuperable. As Kadish concludes, "the unflinching empathy" bound up with writing and reading literature allows us "to spot signs of humanity" where we least expect them. While I don't want to overstate this outcome, I don't want to minimize it, either. Recognizing signs of humanity in our ideological opponents does not magically rebuild torn-apart societies. But it does plant a seed. It keeps alive the possibility of dialogue and connection, slowing down the urge to write off someone else as incorrigible, not worth our time or effort, much as in Smith's story when Alsana and Neena back off from the escalating war of words that is threatening their relationship. As Kadish concludes, recalling Allen's argument in *Talking to Strangers*, acknowledging signs of humanity where we resist finding them "can teach us to start a conversation with the strangest of strangers, to thrive alongside difference," "to become invested in these people, which is very different from agreeing with or even liking them." Engaging with literature, in this case by doing an exercise in a creative writing class, is capable of delivering exactly what American democracy needs.

I have been focusing on the solitary activities of reading and writing works of literature. Discussing works of literature with others only adds to their value in strengthening connections among people even when they hold opposed points of view. The poet Samuel Taylor Coleridge once said that writing poetry brings our whole soul into activity. I would say the same about reading literature. It calls on more of who we are than many other experiences we encounter or things we do. As a result, there is a personal dimension to discussing works of literature that naturally ties us to the people we are discussing them with, even when we disagree with those people. I agree with the literary critic Robert Chodat, who suggests that "artworks elicit an intimacy among audience members that isn't found with most . . . other objects we meet." Chodat goes on to point out, "It's not an accident that new friends and lovers test each other out with gifts of poems, music, or art." Sharing what we enjoy in a work of literature or art tells others who we are and what we care about.

Discussing literature and the arts is more self-revealing, more promising as a springboard to friendship, than discussing many other topics.

In these discussions, we want to know what others think, and we are constantly feeling out what responses we share, where we part company, when we remain unsure of what we think. The very process of trying out our readings on others can fortify our connections with them regardless of any conclusions we arrive at or any differences that arise. A vibrant discussion of literature can create bonds that keep us talking with one another even after we've put down our books. As evidence for this assertion, I would cite the proliferation of book clubs attracting readers of all ages and backgrounds. I see these clubs as providing an experience of community in a polarized society where distrust and loneliness are on the rise. I find it heartening that during the pandemic, when it was especially difficult to maintain our ties to others, some high schools and colleges created book clubs to offset the isolation students were feeling. My point is that these were *book* clubs. They drew on the capacity of literary works to stimulate discussions that strengthen our connections with one another, even when we disagree.

As with attempts to restrict access to reading works of literature, attempts at curtailing discussions of literature testify to their power, as when some legislators and governors claim to be protecting students, especially children, from discussing contentious topics in class, or so-called "divisive concepts," that presumably expose these students to harm. These officials tap into fears they themselves have whipped up by concocting extreme positions and pinning them on their foes. If parents believe that discussing LGBQT characters in works of literature creates opportunities for predators to groom their children, they will be grateful for "Don't Say Gay Laws" promulgated by a forceful governor. The classroom becomes still another space where disagreement feels dangerous, further undermining confidence in discussion and weakening the democracy these students will inherit.

I am not saying that book clubs and literature classes will solve all our problems. I am saying they are valuable. They keep alive an experience of constructive discussion that is under siege elsewhere. I would go so far as to say that these discussions provide a lifeline to an alternative kind of community, a reminder of what we should expect in our workplaces, political culture, and other settings. Expanding that community will require hard, sustained work on many fronts. But institutional change and civic education can work hand in hand and reinforce each other. Reading, creating, and discussing works of literature should play a central role in that education. Learning to share the world with others, whether in a literature classroom, creative writing workshop, or reading group, can result in a cascade of goodwill carrying over into the rest of our lives. If hatred can gather momentum and spread, so can compassion and understanding. The future of our democracy depends on it.

Further Reading

On Democracy

Allen, Danielle. *Justice by Means of Democracy*. Chicago: University of Chicago Press, 2023.

———. *Talking to Strangers: Anxieties of Citizenship since* Brown v. Board of Education. Chicago: University of Chicago Press, 2002.

Applebaum, Anne. *Twilight of Democracy: The Seductive Lure of Authoritarianism*. New York: Doubleday, 2020.

Arendt, Hannah. *The Human Condition*. Chicago: University of Chicago Press, 1958.

Commission on the Practice of Democratic Citizenship. *Our Common Purpose: Reinventing American Democracy for the 21st Century*. Cambridge,

Mass.: American Academy of Arts and Sciences, 2020.

Lefebvre, Alexandre. *Liberalism as a Way of Life*. Princeton: Princeton University Press, 2024.

Levitsky, Steven, and Daniel Ziblatt. *How Democracies Die*. New York: Crown, 2018.

Mason, Lilliana. *Uncivil Agreement: How Politics Became Our Identity*. Chicago: University of Chicago Press, 2018.

Müller, Jan-Werner. *Democracy Rules*. New York: Farrar, Straus and Giroux, 2021.

Tocqueville, Alexis de. *Democracy in America*, ed. Phillips Bradley, trans. Henry Reeve, vol. 1. New York: Doubleday, 1954.

Zerilli, Linda M. G. *A Democratic Theory of Judgment*. Chicago: University of Chicago Press, 2016.

On Polarization and Compromise

Claven, Erik, Robert A. Bush, and Judith A. Saul. "Living with No: Polarization and Transformative Dialogue." *Journal of Dispute Resolution* 2018, no. 1 (2018): 53–63.

Coleman, Peter T. *The Way Out: How to Overcome Toxic Polarization*. New York: Columbia University Press, 2021.

Gutman, Amy, and Dennis Thompson. *The Spirit of Compromise: Why Governing Demands It and Campaigning Undermines It*. Princeton: Princeton University Press, 2012.

Klein, Ezra. *Why We're Polarized*. New York: Avid Reader Press, 2020.

Lawson, April. "Building Trust across the Political Divide: The Surprising Bridge of Conflict." *Comment* 39 (2021): 8–17.

Margalit, Avishai. *On Compromise and Rotten Compromises*. Princeton: Princeton University Press, 2010.

Mnookin, Robert. *Bargaining with the Devil: When to Negotiate, When to Fight*. New York: Simon & Schuster, 2020.

On Literature

Brorby, Taylor. "The Real Reason North Dakota Is Going After Books and Libraries." *New York Times*, February 27, 2023, A19.

Chodat, Robert. "Experts and Encounters." *PMLA* 125 (2020): 989–94.

Fischer, Michael. "Dealing with Disappointment in Democracy." *Athenaeum Review* 5 (2021): 164–81.

———. "Literature and Empathy." *Philosophy and Literature* 41 (2017): 431–64.

———. "Redeeming Disagreement: Lessons Learned from Literary Criticism." *College English* 86 (2023): 36–58.

———. "Ted Cohen on Sharing the World." *Philosophy and Literature* 44 (2020): 188–98.

Hillygus, Sunshine. "The Missing Link: Exploring the Relationship between Higher Education and Political Engagement." *Political Behavior* 27 (2005): 25–47.

Kadish, Rachel. "The Most Important Writing Exercise I've Ever Assigned." *New York Times*, February 23, 2024, A20.

Kean, Susan. *Empathy and the Novel*. Oxford: Oxford University Press, 2007.

Kidd, David Corner, and Emanuele Castan. "Reading Literary Fiction Improves Theory of Mind." *Science* 342 (2013): 377–80.

Nussbaum, Martha. *Love's Knowledge*. Oxford: Oxford University Press, 1990.

———. *Not for Profit: Why Democracy Needs the Humanities*. Princeton: Princeton University Press, 2010.

Further Reading

Scarry, Elaine. "Poetry, Injury, and the Ethics of Reading." In *The Humanities and Public Life*, ed. Peter Brooks with Hilary Jewett, 41–48. New York: Fordham University Press, 2014.

Smith, Zadie. "The Waiter's Wife" (1999). In *The Norton Anthology of English Literature: The Twentieth and Twenty-First Centuries*, ed. Stephen Greenblatt, 10th ed. New York: W. W. Norton, 2018, 1236–48.

Stone, Simone, and Jessie Mae Maimone. "Crafting a Pandemic Book Club." *Library Quarterly: Information, Community, Policy* 94 (2024): 202–18.

Acknowledgments

I especially want to thank Burgin Streetman for urging me to undertake this project and for providing helpful advice along the way. In August 2017 Trinity University president Danny Anderson appointed me the inaugural Janet S. Dicke Professor in Public Humanities, which encouraged me to think about the issues I take up in this book. I am grateful to President Anderson and to Janet and Jim Dicke, not only for creating this professorship but for their many other exceptional contributions to Trinity.

In conjunction with this professorship, in spring 2019 I gave a public lecture at Trinity on "Why Democracy Needs the Humanities." That same semester my colleague Claudia Stokes, then chair of the English department, encouraged me to teach a special seminar on the humanities and democracy, in which I first tried out some of the ideas that I incorporated in my public lecture and have further developed in this book. I want to thank Claudia for her support of that seminar, along with the Trinity faculty members from several departments who visited the class.

I have dedicated this book to my grandchildren, William and Vivian, who at ages seven and four already enjoy checking out books from their nearby public library. I like to think of them engaging in what Thoreau called the noble exercise of reading.

Michael Fischer is the Janet S. Dicke Professor in Public Humanities at Trinity University. He is the author of *Stanley Cavell and Literary Skepticism* and other books on literature and literary criticism. His most recent work explores how philosophy and literature can cultivate the values that sustain healthy democracies and has appeared in *College English*, *Philosophy and Literature*, and elsewhere. He lives in San Antonio, Texas.

www.ingramcontent.com/pod-product-compliance
Lightning Source LLC
Chambersburg PA
CBHW052131030426
42337CB00028B/5107